COLORS and PATTERNS!

by Sarah L. Schuette

A **SPOT-IT, LEARN-IT** CHALLENGE

A+ books

CAPSTONE PRESS
a capstone imprint

A+ Books are published by Capstone Press,
1710 Roe Crest Drive, North Mankato, Minnesota 56003
www.capstonepub.com

Library of Congress Cataloging-in-Publication Data
Cataloging-in-publication information is on file with the Library of Congress.
ISBN 978-1-4765-5109-8 (board book)
ISBN 978-1-4765-5946-9 (eBook PDF)
ISBN 978-1-4765-4011-5 (library binding)
ISBN 978-1-4765-5101-2 (paperback)

Editorial Credits
Jeni Wittrock, editor; Juliette Peters, designer; Wanda Winch, media researcher;
Eric Manske, production specialist; Sarah Schuette, photo stylist; Marcy Morin,
photo scheduler

The author dedicates this book to her Goddaughter Muriel Hilgers.

Photo Credits
all photos by Capstone Studio/Karon Dubke

Note to Parents, Teachers, and Librarians
Spot It, Learn It is an interactive series that supports literacy development and reading
enjoyment. Readers utilize visual discrimination skills to find objects among fun-to-
peruse photographs with busy backgrounds. Readers also build vocabulary through
thematic groupings, develop visual memory ability through repeated readings, and
improve strategic and associative thinking skills by experimenting with different
visual search methods.

Printed in the United States of America in Stevens Point, Wisconsin.
092013   00007773WZS14

Table of Contents

School Time

Can you see a **yellow sea star**?

How many **yellow bees** do you see?

Spot a **gold crown**.

Now find a **yellow pineapple**.

Look for a **yellow hard hat**.

Count the **red stop signs**.

Stars and Stripes

How many **red, white, and blue flags** do you see?

Spot a **striped hot air balloon**.

Count the **gold stars**.

Find a **brown pretzel**.

Look for a **blue butterfly**.

Can you find a **green alien**?

Flamingos

Do you see a **pink fly**?

Find a **pink triangle**.

Spot a **black letter G**.

Now where is a **pink pig**?

Can you see a **ball with polka dots**?

How many **pink stars** do you see?

Orange

Spot a **blue fish**.

Count the **orange buttons**.

Try to find a **green palm tree**.

Now find an **orange fish**.

Look for a **tan taco**.

Where is the **pizza slice with polka dots**?

The Herd!

Try to find a **silver dime**.

Count the **gray elephants**.

Now count the **white tusks**.

Can you see a **brown alligator**?

Where's a **black number 3**?

Spot a **pliers with a red handle**.

Cups

Do you see a **purple seashell**?

Try to find a **red arrow**.

Look for the **green bowling pin**.

Spot the **pink jellyfish**.

Where is the **yellow tennis ball**?

Next spot a **purple scissors**.

Pirate Party

Spot a **green octopus**.

Try to find a **fish with red and white stripes**.

Spot a **blue pen**.

Now find a **black key**.

Look for a **yellow duckling**.

Where is a **white ghost**?

Winter Wonderland

Try to find a **blue football helmet**.

Count the **silver ornaments**.

Can you see a **blue eraser**?

Where's a **green leaf**?

How many **dots on the blue dice**?

Look for all the **white snowflakes**.

Polka Dots

Where's a **blue lizard**?

Find a **brown lantern**.

Spot **2 pink pigs**.

Try to spot a
polka-dot bow tie.

Can you see a
green shamrock?

How many **green
tractors** do you see?

21

Hockey

Spot an **orange ruler**.

Try to find a
blue letter B.

Count the **black
hockey pucks**.

What **colors** are the
other hockey pucks?

Look for a
silver dragonfly.

Where is a
white sheep?

23

Cookies

Count all of the **yellow cookies**.

Find two **pink high-heeled shoes**.

Can you see a **red golf tee**?

Where's a **brown hotdog**?

Spot a **cookie with green dots**.

Find an **orange K**.

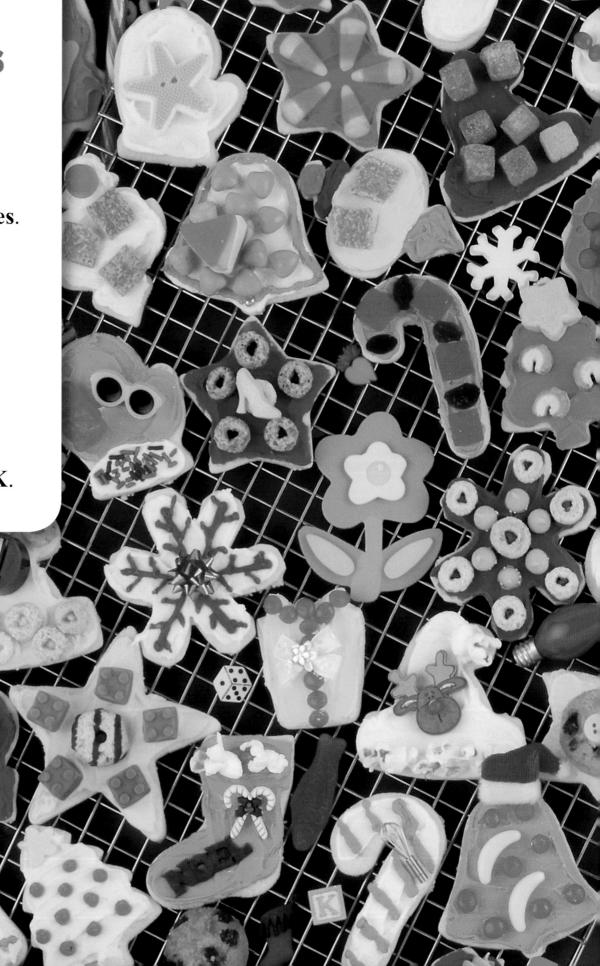

Rainbow

Where's a **red rose**?

Find a **green sailboat**.

Spot an **orange spider**.

Search for a **blue van**.

Can you see a
yellow plane?

What are the colors
on the **candy corn**?

Spot Even More

School Time • page 4

Where is a **pink rabbit**? Try to spot **3 yellow lions**. Can you find a **yellow fork**? Search for an **orange pumpkin**.

Stars and Stripes • page 6

Count the **yellow bananas**. Now spot a **brown safari hat**. Find a **green cactus**. Where's a **white ice cream cone**?

Flamingos • page 8

Spot a **black letter V**. Now find a **turtle with a green head**. Look for a **gray hippo**. Where is a **white paper clip**?

Orange • page 10

Find a **silver star**. Try to find a **purple birthday candle**. Where is a **red basketball player**? Count the **gold trophies**.

The Herd! • page 12

See if you can find a **gray stingray**. Look for a **hammer with polka dots**. Now search for a **gray trumpet**. Where is a **gray dragon**?

Cups • page 14

Do you see a **brown samurai**? Try to find a **watermelon with stripes**. Where is a **black A**? Now look for a **purple shovel**.

Pirate Party • page 16

Can you see a **red fire hydrant**? Count the **gold coins**. Look for a **gray koala**. Try to find a **brown chair**.

Winter Wonderland • page 18

Find a **red letter E**. Where is a **white bone**? Can you count all the **blue birds**? Spot a **blue push pin**.

Polka Dots • page 20

Can you spot a **blue cupcake**? What color is the **pencil**? Count the **dots on the sock**. Find all of the **orange circles**.

Hockey • page 22

Where is a **green owl**? Find a **black fishing pole**. Do you see a **white fence**? Now spot a **blue paintbrush**.

Cookies • page 24

How many **candy canes** do you see? Try to find a **green frog**. What color are the **frog's legs**? Count the **blue stars**.

Rainbow • page 26

Spot a **blue mitten**. Now find a **red anchor**. Look for a **black number 8**. Where is a **green sea turtle**?

Extreme Challenge

Just can't get enough Spot-It action? Here's an extra challenge.

Count all of the **pink dots**.

Spot a **black and white checkered flag**.

What color is the **belt buckle**?

Find a **brown broom**.

What color is the **monkey's tie**?

Do you see a **white swan**?

Spot the **black stripes on a tiger**.

What color is the **construction worker's hat**?

Now where is a **dark blue letter R**?

Can you find a **silver star magic wand**?

What color is the **soccer ball**?

What color is the **unicorn's tail**?

Read More

Adamson, Heather. *Blue.* Colors in Nature. Minneapolis: Bullfrog Books, 2014.

Ghigna, Charles. *The Wonders of the Color Wheel.* My Little School House. North Mankato, Minn.: Picture Window Books, 2014.

Schuette, Sarah L. *Color Camouflage: A Spot-It Challenge.* Spot It. Mankato, Minn.: Capstone Press, 2011.

Internet Sites

FactHound offers a safe, fun way to find Internet sites related to this book. All of the sites on FactHound have been researched by our staff.

Here's all you do:

Visit *www.facthound.com*

Type in this code: 9781476540115

Super-cool stuff! Check out projects, games and lots more at
www.capstonekids.com